BY ALLAN MOREY

THE CINCINNATI
BENGALS
STORY

THE BR
2 PAPER
ROSLYN, NY

BELLWETHER MEDIA · MINNEAPOLIS, MN

Are you ready to take it to the extreme? Torque books thrust you into the action-packed world of sports, vehicles, mystery, and adventure. These books may include dirt, smoke, fire, and chilling tales. **WARNING**: read at your own risk.

This edition first published in 2017 by Bellwether Media, Inc.

No part of this publication may be reproduced in whole or in part without written permission of the publisher. For information regarding permission, write to Bellwether Media, Inc., Attention: Permissions Department, 5357 Penn Avenue South, Minneapolis, MN 55419.

Library of Congress Cataloging-in-Publication Data

Names: Morey, Allan.
Title: The Cincinnati Bengals Story / by Allan Morey.
Description: Minneapolis, MN : Bellwether Media, Inc., 2017. | Series:
    Torque: NFL Teams | Includes index. | Audience: Ages: 7-12. | Audience:
    Grades: 3 through 7.
Identifiers: LCCN 2015045881 | ISBN 9781626173613 (hardcover : alk. paper)
Subjects: LCSH: Cincinnati Bengals (Football team)–History–Juvenile literature.
Classification: LCC GV956.C54 M69 2017 | DDC 796.332/640977178–dc23
LC record available at http://lccn.loc.gov/2015045881

Printed in the United States of America, North Mankato, MN.

TABLE OF CONTENTS

HEADED TO THE PLAYOFFS 4

PASSING ATTACK 8

THEN TO NOW 14

BENGALS TIMELINE 18

TEAM SUPERSTARS 20

FANS AND TEAM CULTURE 24

MORE ABOUT THE BENGALS 28

GLOSSARY 30

TO LEARN MORE 31

INDEX 32

It is the last game of the 2015 regular season. The Cincinnati Bengals face the Baltimore Ravens.

Marvin Jones

AJ
McCarron

The Ravens score first. They kick two field goals. Then the Bengals push down the field. **Quarterback** AJ McCarron tosses a touchdown pass to **tight end** Tyler Eifert! But the Ravens kick another field goal before the half.

Jeremy Hill

In the third quarter, McCarron throws a short pass to **wide receiver** A.J. Green. Touchdown! Minutes later, **running back** Jeremy Hill rumbles into the end zone for another touchdown.

The Bengals go on to win the game. They are in the **playoffs**!

SCORING TERMS

END ZONE

the area at each end of a football field; a team scores by entering the opponent's end zone with the football.

EXTRA POINT

a score that occurs when a kicker kicks the ball between the opponent's goal posts after a touchdown is scored; 1 point.

FIELD GOAL

a score that occurs when a kicker kicks the ball between the opponent's goal posts; 3 points.

SAFETY

a score that occurs when a player on offense is tackled behind his own goal line; 2 points for defense.

TOUCHDOWN

a score that occurs when a team crosses into its opponent's end zone with the football; 6 points.

TWO-POINT CONVERSION

a score that occurs when a team crosses into its opponent's end zone with the football after scoring a touchdown; 2 points.

The Bengals have long been known for a strong passing attack. In the 1980s, they developed a new "no-huddle" **offense**. Players did not stop to huddle up between plays. Their fast pace tired out **defenses**.

1981 season

8

Bill
Walsh

The "West Coast" offense was also developed in Cincinnati. Former assistant coach Bill Walsh built the style. It favors passing and is about timing and speed.

Cincinnati is in southwestern Ohio. It lies along the Ohio River near Kentucky. This is why many Kentuckians also cheer for the Bengals.

The Bengals call Paul Brown Stadium their home. It is named after the team's first head coach.

JUNGLE CATS
Wild Bengal tigers live in the jungle. Fans nicknamed Paul Brown Stadium "The Jungle."

PAUL BROWN STADIUM

CINCINNATI, OHIO

The Bengals joined the National Football League (NFL) in 1970. They play in the American Football **Conference** (AFC). They are part of the North **Division**.

The Pittsburgh Steelers, Cleveland Browns, and Baltimore Ravens are the other teams in the North Division. The Browns are big in-state **rivals**.

NFL DIVISIONS

AFC

AFC NORTH
- BALTIMORE RAVENS
- CINCINNATI BENGALS
- CLEVELAND BROWNS
- PITTSBURGH STEELERS

AFC EAST
- BUFFALO BILLS
- MIAMI DOLPHINS
- NEW ENGLAND PATRIOTS
- NEW YORK JETS

AFC SOUTH
- HOUSTON TEXANS
- INDIANAPOLIS COLTS
- JACKSONVILLE JAGUARS
- TENNESSEE TITANS

AFC WEST
- DENVER BRONCOS
- KANSAS CITY CHIEFS
- OAKLAND RAIDERS
- SAN DIEGO CHARGERS

NFC

NFC NORTH

 CHICAGO
BEARS

 DETROIT
LIONS

 GREEN BAY
PACKERS

 MINNESOTA
VIKINGS

NFC EAST

 DALLAS
COWBOYS

 NEW YORK
GIANTS

 PHILADELPHIA
EAGLES

 WASHINGTON
REDSKINS

NFC SOUTH

 ATLANTA
FALCONS

 CAROLINA
PANTHERS

 NEW ORLEANS
SAINTS

 TAMPA BAY
BUCCANEERS

NFC WEST

 ARIZONA
CARDINALS

 LOS ANGELES
RAMS

 SAN FRANCISCO
49ERS

 SEATTLE
SEAHAWKS

The Bengals formed as a team in the American Football League (AFL). Paul Brown helped start the team in 1968. He was the former coach of the Browns.

Paul Brown

1973
season

In 1970, AFL teams joined the NFL. The Bengals won their first NFL division title that season. They won another one in 1973.

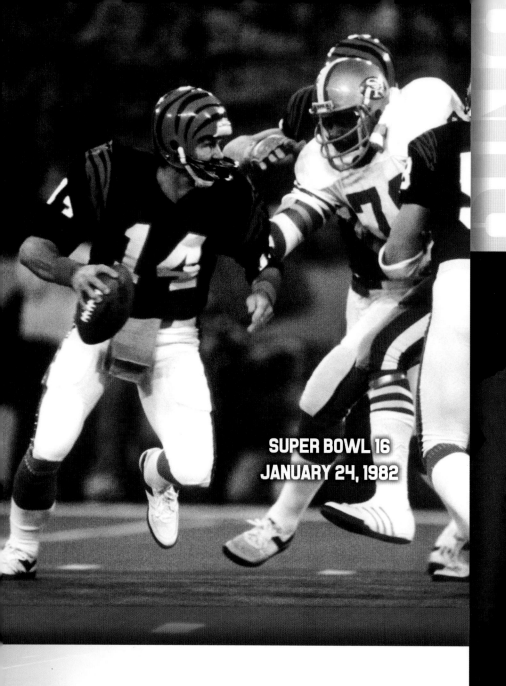

SUPER BOWL 16
JANUARY 24, 1982

In the 1980s, the Bengals played
in the **Super Bowl** twice. Both times
they lost to the San Francisco 49ers.

The 1990s and 2000s were tough years. The team often struggled to make the playoffs. But they have had some recent success. Starting in 2011, they have made the playoffs several seasons in a row.

2015
season

BENGALS
TIMELINE

1968
Formed as an AFL team

1975
Celebrated Coach Paul Brown's retirement

1984
Drafted quarterback Boomer Esiason

1970
Joined the NFL

1982
Played in Super Bowl 16, but lost to the San Francisco 49ers

21 FINAL SCORE **26**

2001

Drafted wide receiver Chad Johnson

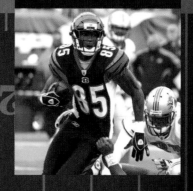

2000

First played in the new Paul Brown Stadium

2002

Joined the AFC's North Division

1989

Played in Super Bowl 23, but lost to the San Francisco 49ers

16 FINAL SCORE **20**

2011

Drafted quarterback Andy Dalton and wide receiver A.J. Green

The Bengals have had some great players on offense. Quarterback Ken Anderson led the team in the 1970s and 1980s. He was a four-time **Pro Bowler**.

Ken Anderson

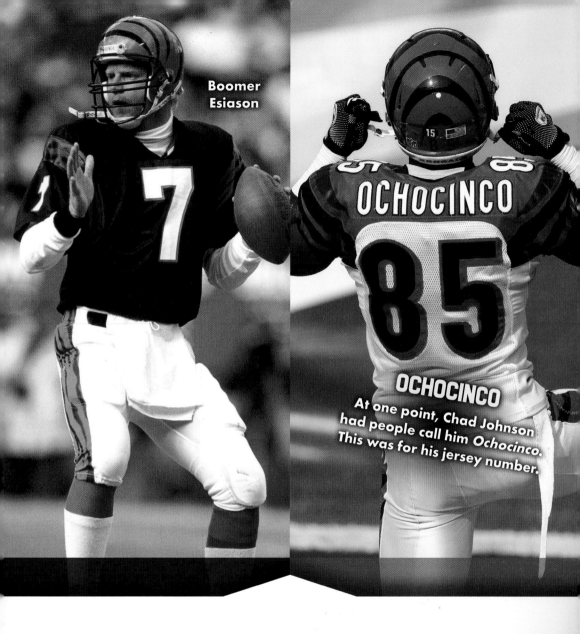

Boomer
Esiason

OCHOCINCO
85
OCHOCINCO

OCHOCINCO
At one point, Chad Johnson had people call him Ochocinco. This was for his jersey number.

Quarterback Boomer Esiason helped shape the "no-huddle" offense. He led the team to Super Bowl 23. In the 2000s, wide receiver Chad Johnson racked up more than 10,000 receiving yards!

Today, the Bengals continue to have stars on offense. Quarterback Andy Dalton is one of the league's best passers. His favorite target is A.J. Green. Green's size and speed make him tough to stop.

On defense, big **defensive lineman** Geno Atkins leads the way. He is quick to stop runs and **sack** quarterbacks.

TEAM GREATS

KEN ANDERSON
QUARTERBACK
1971-1986

BOOMER ESIASON
QUARTERBACK
1984-1992, 1997

CHAD JOHNSON
WIDE RECEIVER
2001-2010

PASSING DUO

Dalton and Green set a record their first year in the league. They connected for 1,057 receiving yards. That is the most ever by a rookie quarterback-receiver combo.

GENO ATKINS
DEFENSIVE TACKLE
2010-PRESENT

ANDY DALTON
QUARTERBACK
2011-PRESENT

A.J. GREEN
WIDE RECEIVER
2011-PRESENT

Paul Brown Stadium is a sea of orange and black on game day. Tiger mascot Who Dey helps get fans excited.

Who Dey

On big plays, the speakers
blast his favorite song, "Welcome
to the Jungle." The fans yell
to make it tough for opposing
players to hear.

The Bengals have yet to win a Super Bowl. But fans still have had a lot to cheer about. Their team has been playing well and making the playoffs often.

Fans also have their team's stars to back. Right now, Dalton and Green give them plenty to roar about!

Team name:
Cincinnati Bengals

Team name explained:
Named after a former pro football team that played from 1937 to 1941

Nickname:
The Orange and Black

Joined NFL: 1970
(AFL from 1968-1969)

Conference: AFC

Division: North

Main rivals: Cleveland Browns, Pittsburgh Steelers

OHIO

CINCINNATI

Home stadium name:
Paul Brown Stadium

Stadium opened: **2000**

Seats in stadium: **65,515**

Name for fan base: **Bengals Nation**

Mascot: **Who Dey**

Logo: **An orange "B" with black stripes, like a Bengal tiger**

Colors: **Black, orange, white**

GLOSSARY

conference—a large grouping of sports teams that often play one another

defenses—groups of players who try to stop opposing teams from scoring

defensive lineman—a player on defense whose main job is to try to stop the quarterback; defensive linemen crouch down in front of the ball.

division—a small grouping of sports teams; usually there are several divisions of teams in a conference.

offense—the group of players who try to move down the field and score

playoffs—the games played after the regular NFL season is over; playoff games determine which teams play in the Super Bowl.

Pro Bowler—a player who makes the Pro Bowl, the NFL's all-star game

quarterback—a player on offense whose main job is to throw and hand off the ball

rivals—teams that are long-standing opponents

running back—a player on offense whose main job is to run with the ball

sack—to tackle the opposing quarterback for a loss of yards

Super Bowl—the championship game for the NFL

tight end—a player on offense whose main jobs are to catch the ball and block for teammates

wide receiver—a player on offense whose main job is to catch passes from the quarterback

TO LEARN MORE

AT THE LIBRARY

Burgess, Zack. *Meet the Cincinnati Bengals*. Chicago, Ill.: Norwood House Press, 2016.

Gigliotti, Jim. *AFC North*. Mankato, Minn.: Child's World, 2012.

Gilbert, Sara. *The Story of the Cincinnati Bengals*. Mankato, Minn.: Creative Education, 2014.

ON THE WEB

Learning more about the Cincinnati Bengals is as easy as 1, 2, 3.

1. Go to www.factsurfer.com.

2. Enter "Cincinnati Bengals" into the search box.

3. Click the "Surf" button and you will see a list of related web sites.

With factsurfer.com, finding more information is just a click away.

INDEX

American Football League (AFL), 14, 15, 28

Brown, Paul (head coach), 10, 14

championship, 15, 16, 21, 26

Cincinnati, Ohio, 9, 10, 11, 29

colors, 24, 29

conference, 12, 13, 28

division, 12, 13, 15, 28

fans, 10, 24, 25, 26, 27, 29

logo, 29

mascot, 24, 29

name, 28

nicknames, 10, 21, 28

"no-huddle" offense, 8, 21

Paul Brown Stadium, 10, 11, 24, 29

players, 4, 5, 6, 8, 20, 21, 22, 23, 25, 27

playoffs, 6, 17, 26

positions, 5, 6, 8, 9, 20, 21, 22, 23

Pro Bowler, 20

record, 23

rivals, 12, 14, 28

scoring terms, 5, 6, 7

Super Bowl, 16, 21, 26

timeline, 18-19

traditions, 24, 25, 26, 27

training camp, 29

vs. Baltimore Ravens (January 3, 2016), 4-7

Walsh, Bill (assistant coach), 9

"West Coast" offense, 9